YOUR KNOWLEDGE HAS VALUE

- We will publish your bachelor's and
  master's thesis, essays and papers

- Your own eBook and book -
  sold worldwide in all relevant shops

- Earn money with each sale

Upload your text at www.GRIN.com
and publish for free

Bibliographic information published by the German National Library:

The German National Library lists this publication in the National Bibliography; detailed bibliographic data are available on the Internet at http://dnb.dnb.de .

This book is copyright material and must not be copied, reproduced, transferred, distributed, leased, licensed or publicly performed or used in any way except as specifically permitted in writing by the publishers, as allowed under the terms and conditions under which it was purchased or as strictly permitted by applicable copyright law. Any unauthorized distribution or use of this text may be a direct infringement of the author s and publisher s rights and those responsible may be liable in law accordingly.

Imprint:

Copyright © 2016 GRIN Verlag, Open Publishing GmbH
Print and binding: Books on Demand GmbH, Norderstedt Germany
ISBN: 9783668334427

This book at GRIN:

http://www.grin.com/en/e-book/342996/the-underground-railroad-and-slavery-in-the-united-states

Bernd Müller-Knospe

The "Underground Railroad" and Slavery in the United States

GRIN Publishing

GRIN - Your knowledge has value

Since its foundation in 1998, GRIN has specialized in publishing academic texts by students, college teachers and other academics as e-book and printed book. The website www.grin.com is an ideal platform for presenting term papers, final papers, scientific essays, dissertations and specialist books.

Visit us on the internet:

http://www.grin.com/

http://www.facebook.com/grincom

http://www.twitter.com/grin_com

The "Underground Railroad" and Slavery in the United States

Remark on the use of the word "Negro" for African Americans: up to the 1960s, this was the word used by white and black Americans to designate Americans of African descent. Even fighters for black equality like Martin L. Kind or Malcolm X used the term "Negro" when speaking of their fellow African Americans. For that reason the term is used throughout this paper.

What was the Underground Railroad (UR)?

The UR "was neither a railroad nor underground, but merely a conviction set to action"[1].

"Was the Underground Railroad truly a nationwide conspiracy with 'conductors', 'agents', and 'depots', or did popular imagination simply construct this figment out of a series of ad hoc, unconnected escapes? Were its principal heroes brave Southern blacks, or sympathetic Northern whites? The answers depend on which historians you believe"[2]

It is easier to say what the Underground Railroad was not than to say what it really was. And any attempt at defining it depends very much on the sources used, as the quotation above indicates.

It was not an organization, not even a network or an established set of routes that slaves could follow. It was rather an ever-changing, but also ever-growing number of options for slaves from the south to escape slavery and to reach the northern states and particularly Canada, the country which would guarantee complete and unrestricted protection from persecution. It consisted of secret paths, safe houses, ways of clandestine communication, various means of transportation, but the most important aspect was the existence and the determination of people who were ready to help their enslaved fellow man or woman to reach a place where they could live in freedom.

And often enough these people – black and white, male and female – risked their own freedom, their belongings and even their lives to help others. Particularly after the adoption of the Fugitive Slave Act of 1850 citizens were running a big risk when they helped Negro slaves, as this law made helping fugitive Negroes a crime.

---

[1] H. Buckmaster, p. 29.
[2] www.theatlantic.com/magazine/archive/2015/03/the-secret-history-of-the-underground-railroad/384966.

Secret escape routes for black slaves started in the 17th century but what today is called the UR began in the early 19th century and reached its peak between 1840 and 1860. According to estimates, about 100,000 slaves escaped to the north in the first half of the 19th century.[3] It ceased to exist after the Emancipation Proclamation of 1862 and the end of the Civil War in 1865.

Most fugitives came from the states bordering the free North. From the more western slave states escape routes mainly lead to the states north of the Ohio river (called "River Jordan" by the slaves): Ohio, Indiana, Illinois, but also to Iowa and Wisconsin.

Routes from states more to the east, like Georgia, the Carolinas and Virginia lead to Pennsylvania and the New England states.

However many fugitives didn't stop there, but continued their flight to Canada, the only really safe place for Negro slaves.

As it was next to impossible to reach the North from Texas, there was an escape route to Mexico. A similar situation existed in Florida, from where most fugitives went to the Caribbean.

Terms and explanations

The term "Underground Railroad" came into use in the 1830. The origin of the term being unknown, there are various stories trying to explain it. One explanation for the "underground" aspect is the following anecdote: The owner of a fugitive slave who had tracked down and almost reached his "possession" had to get a boat to follow him across the river into which the desperate Negro had jumped, this being his only chance to escape his hunters. While the people who were with the slave holder organized the boat, the gentleman never lost sight of his prey, but when the slave had reached the opposite shore, he suddenly disappeared. After crossing the river, the slave owner tried everything possible to find the slave, but without success. This allegedly led him to the only explanation possible: "'he must have gone on an underground road'".[4]

Railroad terms were used to describe the system, as the railroad was the emerging transportation system of the day. Safe places were called "stations", run by "station masters", who gave information called "tickets" to their prospective "packages" or "freight", with

[3] http://teacher.scholastic.com/activities/bhistory/underground_railroad/myths.htm.
[4] H. Buckmaster, p. 59.

"conductors" guiding them on secret "lines". "Stockholders" were people who supported the system with money or supplies.[5] An important aspect of help by "stockholders" was that they often donated clothing so that fugitives who travelled by boat or on real trains did not have to wear their work clothes and could therefore not easily be detected.[6]

Traveling conditions, organization

Running away was a risky and very dangerous endeavor, for long distances had to be covered, help was scarce despite the existence of the UR and often the Negroes had to rely on their own resources, at least at the beginning of their flight. There was the constant threat of the slave master trying to get back his "possession", either by going after the runaway himself or by using professional slave hunters who even followed him or her into the free Northern states.

What added to their difficulties was that Negroes in the South were often kept in complete ignorance by their masters, they normally didn't get any school education, most of them could not read or write, they hardly ever left their farm or only knew the immediate surroundings of the place where they lived and worked. So finding their way to places hundreds of miles away was an enormous challenge for them. 'Follow the North Star' was the only information that many of them had.

Once their getaway had been successful, most of the time the slaves walked at night, about 10 to 20 miles to the next "station", if possible. There they would rest and eat, often hidden in basements, barns or attics until the next "conductor" would lead them to another "station".

Sometimes white people or light-skinned Negroes would lead a group of fugitives, posing as a slave master leading their slaves in some kind of business. They would even travel by ship or by railroad. If that was not possible, fugitives would sometimes be transported on wagons with false bottoms or hidden under layers of straw.[7]

Some runaways stayed close to their farms, lived on hunting, fishing or stealing food from neighboring farms, often supported by their fellow-slaves who looked the other way. There were even slaves who fled to the nearest mountains, to remote places like the bayous of

---

[5] www.haworthassociation.org.
[6] www.historynet.com/underground-railroad.
[7] www.haworthassociation.org.

Louisiana, built houses and started farming in faraway, inaccessible areas inside the slave states. [8]

To reduce the risk of infiltration, many people associated with the Underground Railroad knew only their part of the operation and not of the whole scheme, for example the way to the next station and the people who would guide the fugitives to their next stop.

And even when the flight was successful, when a Northern state was reached, the slave's trouble was not over. Although they were no longer slaves, they were not accepted as equals by white society and racism was widespread. The Blacks' worst enemies were poor Whites who saw them first of all as competitors for jobs.

Supporters of the Underground Railroad:

Here are three examples of famous Americans supporting the Abolitionist movement and the UR. The choice is of course random, as there are hundreds or even thousands of people who helped their fellow human beings in the most unselfish and courageous way and would merit to be mentioned.

Harriet Tubman

Harriet Tubman was an American slave who escaped from the South and who became a leading Abolitionist and perhaps the most well-known "conductor" of the Underground Railroad before the American Civil War. She was born in Maryland in the early 1820s, and successfully escaped in 1849 to Philadelphia. But she returned at least 13 times [9] to rescue first her own family members and later other slaves. She led hundreds to freedom in the North on the Underground Railroad, with figures varying greatly from 70 to 300 people, according to the source which is consulted. This earned her the nickname of the "Moses" of her people. There are several reports saying that on her missions she always carried a handgun to defend herself against dogs or slave catchers and which she also used to threaten anyone who wanted to turn back. She allegedly told them: "you'll be free or you die". [10] She was so successful as a "conductor", that by 1856 a $40,000 reward was put on her head. In the Civil War she worked for the Union in various jobs, as a cook, a nurse and sometimes even as a spy. After the Civil War she settled in Auburn, N.Y. Tubman died in 1913.

---

[8] H. Buckmaster, p. 17.
[9] other sources speak of 19 returns, f.ex. http://www.ushistory.org/us/28c.asp.
[10] http://www.pbs.org/wgbh/aia/part4/4p1535.html.

In April 2016, the U.S. Treasury Department announced that Harriet Tubman will replace Andrew Jackson, an American President and a slaveholder, on the center of a new $20 bill. In 2008 a bronze statue of Tubman, created by African-American artist Alison Saar was unveiled in Manhattan.

William Still

William Still, a free-born Black, became an Abolitionist movement leader and writer during the antebellum period in American history. He was also one of the most successful Black businessmen in the history of the City of Philadelphia. Born in 1821, in Burlington County, New Jersey, he was the youngest of eighteen children of Levin and Charity Still. Both of his parents were born into slavery. His father bought his freedom and his mother escaped slavery in Maryland. William Still grew up with vivid images of the horrors of slavery. His parents instilled in him strong family and work values as well as pride and self-determination. In 1844, he moved to Philadelphia and in 1847 married Letitia George, who gave birth to their four children. That year, he was hired as clerk for the Pennsylvania Society for the Abolition of Slavery. He became an active agent on the Underground Railroad, assisting fugitive Africans who came to Philadelphia. With the passage of the Fugitive Slave Act of 1850, Still was appointed chairman of the society's Vigilance Committee that aided and supported fugitive Africans.

William Still is best known for his book "The Underground Railroad" (1872) where he documented the stories of enslaved African-Americans who won their freedom by escaping from slavery, many with the help of the UR.[11]

Levi Coffin – Catherine Coffin

The Coffins were North Carolina Quakers who dedicated their lives to helping enslaved men and women escape slavery. They claimed to have helped some 3,000 men and women flee slavery. Because of his efforts, Coffin became known as "the President of the Underground Railroad." As a child he was taught that slavery was evil and living in a slave state he witnessed the reality of slavery himself.

In the early 1820s, Coffin and a relative started a Sunday school to teach slaves to read the Bible. The plan was short-lived though, as they were soon forced by slaveholders to close the

---

[11] http://stillfamily.library.temple.edu/historical-perspective/william-still-significance.

school.[12] In 1826 the Coffins, like thousands of other Quakers, moved to Newport in free Indiana (now Fountain City), as they did not want to live in a state that permitted slavery and as in North Carolina Quakers were persecuted by slaveholders. With supporters of the Abolitionist movement and a number of fugitive slaves living in the town and because of the fact that it was at the intersection of main roads it was an ideal theatre for a "station" of the UR. Their eight-room home was a famous safe haven for fugitive slaves on the UR and was often called the "Grand Central Station of the Underground Railroad" [13].

Levi Coffin was born in 1798 in North Carolina. As a young boy he saw the horrors of slavery firsthand and later on his religious beliefs made him even resist the law. He is quoted as saying that he had "to obey God's law, not man's law". [14] He was a successful businessman as a farmer and as a merchant, which allowed him to provide the money needed to supply food, clothes and transportation for the UR in his area.[15]

In 1847 the Coffins moved to Cincinnati and Levi opened a warehouse that sold only goods produced by free labor. The Coffins also kept helping fugitive slaves and after the end of the Civil War Levi Coffin raised money in America and even in Europe to help African Americans start a business.[16]

"The Coffin house was purchased in 1967 by the State of Indiana. The house was restored and then opened to the public in 1970" [17] and it is now a registered National Historic Landmark.

Historical Background

When America was first colonized by Europeans, there was a severe shortage of labor. So-called indentured servants, people who could not afford to pay for the passage from Europe to America, paid off their passage through their work and then became free men. But their numbers were insufficient and so when in 1619 a Dutch ship with African slaves arrived in Virginia, this seemed to be the solution to the labor shortage problem.

At the beginning sometimes Africans arriving in North America were treated like the white indentured servants. But by and by conditions changed for Africans until by the middle of the 18th century they were treated as 'chattel slaves', personal property of their owners, quite like

---

[12] http://docsouth.unc.edu/nc/coffin/bio.html.
[13] https://www.indianalandmarks.org/levi-coffin-and-the-underground-railroad.
[14] http://www.aaregistry.org/historic_events/view/levi-coffin-underground-railroad-ambassador.
[15] http://www.waynet.org/levicoffin.
[16] http://www.learnnc.org/lp/editions/nchist-antebellum/4739.
[17] http://www.waynet.org/levicoffin.

any other personal belonging, f.ex. a horse or a cow. They could be bought and sold or mortgaged like a house or like furniture.

Out of the approximately 11 million Africans who were brought to the Americas as slaves, only about 400,000 were taken to North America plus about 80,000 who arrived there via the Caribbean. Most of them went to the Caribbean and to South America, particularly to Brazil, with about 5 million African slaves the biggest market of the slave trade.

In the United States there was a divide between North and South. There were also slaves in the North, but most of them were taken to farms in the South, as southern cash crops – tobacco, rice and cotton – were very labor-intensive and as there were no machines at the time, this required a large human workforce.

Not all slave owners were cruel and sadistic, most of them treated their slaves humanely, but families were often separated, men, women and children were frequently sold away from one another and corporal punishment was considered to be normal. Africans were regarded as an inferior race and even the Supreme Court ruled in its infamous Dred Scott Decision that Black slaves "were subhuman property with no rights of citizenship."[18] The law did not protect Black slaves and they had no chance to protest against their treatment, quite apart from the fact, that every farm was its own little 'kingdom' with its own rules, that no one from the outside could control.

But many slaves were not ready to accept a life in bondage and ran away. And as a slave represented valuable property, the slave owners tried to prevent this. That is why in 1793 the first Fugitive Slave Act was passed by Congress. The government in Washington gave local authorities the power to capture runaway slaves and take them back to their owners. Unfortunately for the slaveholders, Northern States largely ignored the law or made it difficult for slave hunters to get hold of their prey. For example in Indiana slave owners had to prove their ownership with written documents and in order to search a house where fugitive slaves were suspected to hide, a search warrant was needed which sometimes was very hard to obtain.

The Southern slavocracy, the upper class of wealthy and politically all-powerful planters and their supporters argued (and maybe even believed) that Black slaves were unable to care for

---

[18] http://www.civilwar.org/education/history/civil-war-overview/slavery.html.

themselves and that slavery was "a benevolent institution that kept them fed, clothed, and occupied".[19]

In the 19th century the conflict between North and South escalated, as public opinion in the North turned more and more against slavery, helped by a growing Abolitionist movement and as the Southern upper class realized more and more clearly that their economy and their whole lifestyle could only be maintained by the system of slavery.

And as between 1800 and 1850 around 100,000 slaves fled to the North with the help of the Underground Railroad [20], tension between slaveholders and those who profited from the system as opposed to those who saw slavery as something vicious that had to be stopped as soon as possible increased constantly.

Other factors which increased the number of runaways were the Dred Scott decision by the Supreme Court and the Fugitive Slave Act of 1850.

Dred Scott was a slave whose master was an army surgeon who had taken him from Missouris for some years to Illinois and Minnesota, a free state. Therefore Dred Scott claimed his freedom, but The Supreme Court decided that Scott's stay of two years to Illinois and the Northwest Territory did not make him a free man. "The Court further ruled that as a black man Scott was excluded from United States citizenship and could not, therefore, bring suit. … African-Americans had not been part of the of the 'sovereign people' who made the Constitution." [21]

The Fugitive Slave Act allowed slave hunters to follow alleged runaway slaves even into free Northern states. They could capture any Black person simply by asserting that he or she was a fugitive slave. The Negro had no right to appeal to a court, which was an incentive to even kidnap free Negroes, pretending they were runaway slaves. Furthermore it obliged all public servants to help slave owners to capture their "possession" and it made obstructing the capture of runaways a crime that could be punished by 6 months in prison and a $1,000 fine.

This of course threatened the safety of all Negroes and greatly increased the numbers fleeing to the North and to Canada.[22]

---

[19] http://www.civilwar.org/education/history/civil-war-overview/slavery.html.
[20] http://www.harriet-tubman.org/interesting-facts-about-the-underground-railroad.

[21] http://www.ushistory.org/us/32a.asp.
[22] https://memory.loc.gov/ammem/aaohtml/exhibit/aopart3b.html.

When after the election of Abraham Lincoln to the Presidency in 1860, the Southern states finally seceded from the Union and established the independent Confederate States of America, this lead to the Civil War, which began as a fight to save the Union and not as one to stop slavery. In 1862, however, President Lincoln issued the Emancipation Proclamation which set slaves in all rebel states free. In 1865 Congress passed the 13th Amendment making slavery illegal in all of the United States.

Economy and slavery

The economy of the South was an agriculture-oriented economy, industry was almost exclusively developing in the Northern states. Cotton, tobacco, rice were the most important products and all of them were extremely labor-intensive. The hot, dry climate of the Southern states was very favorable to the growing of cotton, which eventually became the dominant cash crop.

The invention of the cotton gin (a term derived from 'engine') by Ely Whitney in 1793 [23] which allowed the cleaning of up to 50 pounds of cotton by one worker in a day instead of just 1 pound done manually [24] and together with the rising demand for ever more cotton in the United States and even more so in Europe, an economic miracle happened. Whereas in 1791 about 9000 bales of cotton had been produced in the South, the figure went up to 1,039,000 bales in 1831. By 1860 'King Cotton', as it was called then represented nearly 60% of all American exports with an overall value of about $200 million per year.

The European Industrial Revolution of the 19th century created the machines that could process large quantities of cotton and clothing made of cotton was much cheaper than traditional handmade products from wool. This led to an ever-growing demand for cotton and gave an enormous boost to the Southern economy. On the other hand it increased the mutual economic dependence between North and South as most of the Southern production was processed in the New England states and as Northern industrialist were heavily invested in the cotton business. "On the eve of the Civil War, New England's economy, so fundamentally dependent upon the textile industry, was inextricably intertwined(...) to the labor of black people working as slaves in the U.S. South." [25]

---

[23] for more details about the invention of the cotton gin and for information about other groundbreaking inventions by Ely Whitney go to: http://www.eliwhitney.org/7/museum/about-eli-whitney/inventor.

[24] http://www.history.com/topics/inventions/cotton-gin-and-eli-whitney.

[25] http://www.pbs.org/wnet/african-americans-many-rivers-to-cross/history/why-was-cotton-king.

One unfortunate consequence of the success of the cotton gin was the strengthening and even the expansion of slavery in the South. It made growing cotton more profitable and thus more cotton was grown. This on the other hand required a larger workforce and so the farmers increased the number of slaves, the cheapest workers they could get. [26]

The economic impact of runaway slaves was often exaggerated, particularly by Southern slaveholders, for political reasons, as the few hundred runaways per year had little consequence for the southern economy. But the psychological effect on the slave population in the South was enormous, as it showed them what was possible if only they had the courage to take their chances. This is why the Southern slavocracy lobbied intensely for stricter laws which would allow them to persecute runaway slave even into the Northern states and thus discourage potential runaways.

Concluding remarks

When arriving at their destinations, many fugitives were disappointed. Life in the North and particularly in Canada was very different, sometimes conditions were very hard, the climate was much colder and often the Negroes were not welcome. Discrimination was widespread as the newly arriving Southerners competed for jobs with poor whites and immigrants from Europe.

When the Civil War broke out, many Blacks joined the Union Army and when slavery was ultimately abolished with the end of the war, thousands of fugitives returned to their former homes to unite with friends and family.

---

[26] http://www.history.com/topics/inventions/cotton-gin-and-eli-whitney.

List of References

Henrietta Buckmaster "Let my People Go: the story of the underground railroad and the growth of the abolition movement" (Boston 1969, first publ. 1941, ISBN 0-8070-5477-1, available at Universitätsbibliothek Essen-Duisburg, Signatur OCE1210)

Online sources:

African-American Registry – Levi Coffin, Underground Railroad Ambassador

http://www.aaregistry.org/historic_events/view/levi-coffin-underground-railroad-ambassador

Civil War Trust – Slavery in the United States

http://www.civilwar.org/education/history/civil-war-overview/slavery.html

Documenting the American South

http://docsouth.unc.edu/nc/coffin/bio.html

Harriet Tubman – Historical Society

http://www.harriet-tubman.org/interesting-facts-about-the-underground-railroad

Haworth Association of America

www.haworthassociation.org

Cotton Gin and Eli Whitney

http://www.history.com/topics/inventions/cotton-gin-and-eli-whitney

Historynet – Underground Railroad

www.historynet.com/underground-railroad

Indiana Landmarks - Levi Coffin and the Underground Railroad

https://www.indianalandmarks.org/levi-coffin-and-the-underground-railroad/

Learn NC – North Carolina digital history

http://www.learnnc.org/lp/editions/nchist-antebellum/4739

African American Odyssey - Abolition, Anti-Slavery Movements, and the Rise of the Sectional Controversy

https://memory.loc.gov/ammem/aaohtml/exhibit/aopart3b.html

Public Broadcasting Service - The African Americans

http://www.pbs.org/wnet/african-americans-many-rivers-to-cross/

William Still

http://stillfamily.library.temple.edu/historical-perspective/william-still-significance

Remark: his book "The Underground Railroad" is available as a free download at the "Project Gutenberg" library.

Myths of the UR

http://teacher.scholastic.com/activities/bhistory/underground_railroad/myths.htm

History of the UR

www.theatlantic.com/magazine/archive/2015/03/the-secret-history-of-the-underground-railroad/384966.

US. History

http://www.ushistory.org/us/32a.asp

Levy Coffin

http://www.waynet.org/levicoffin/

Other sources of information on the UR:

Maps showing escape routes :

http://nationalgeographic.org/activity/underground-railroad-route/

Presentations:

A "Prezi" presentation on the UR can be found at:

https://prezi.com/qgwimfzopszz/the-underground-railroad/

YOUR KNOWLEDGE HAS VALUE

- We will publish your bachelor's and
  master's thesis, essays and papers

- Your own eBook and book -
  sold worldwide in all relevant shops

- Earn money with each sale

Upload your text at www.GRIN.com
and publish for free